Shifted Voices

Zanae Demery

BookLeaf Publishing

India | USA | UK

Shifted Voices © 2024 Zanae Demery

All rights reserved.

No part of this publication may be reproduced, stored in a retrieval system, or transmitted, in any form or by any means, electronic, mechanical, photocopying, recording or otherwise, without the prior written permission of the presenters.

Zanae Demery asserts the moral right to be identified as author of this work.

Presentation by *BookLeaf Publishing*

Web: www.bookleafpub.com

E-mail: info@bookleafpub.com

ISBN: 9789360944193

First edition 2024

I dedicate this book to all the foster kids, the black sheeps of the family, or just anyone who's ever known that deep pain and grief. This is your healing.

ACKNOWLEDGEMENT

I would like to acknowledge my mentor Kacey, my sister's and brothers , and my wonderful partner Ryan.

PREFACE

In this collection of poetry, each piece is a fragment of life—my life, and the lives of those who have crossed my path. These verses are born from moments of joy and sorrow, encounters that left imprints on the soul, and the everyday musings that connect us all. Through these poems, I invite you to glimpse the world through my eyes, and perhaps see reflections of your own experiences. It is my deepest hope that within these pages, you will find a resonance, a comfort, or a spark that ignites your own journey of expression.

The Girl With The Silent Yell

The girl with the silent yell
Had a story too big to tell
Tired of playing this game of song and dance
The girl with the silent yell never stood a chance
Compresse in a soundproof room
Destined to an unfair doom
Her chords are moving but no words are being
released
Can anyone help her please
She wears the marks of every defeat
If only her call out was able to be reached
THERE GOES THE YELL no one is coming
THERE GOES THE YELL from the unwanted
loving
THERE GOES THE YELL she can't do it
anymore
THERE GOES THE YELL and all her tears on
the floor
THERE GOES THE…nothing the yell is gone
Because she no longer knew what she was
waiting on
A savior? No those don't exist
There is no more yell and the girl has perished

The girl with the silent yell that everyone knows
and sees
The girl with the silent yell..that girl is me

Misunderstanding

I'll never understand why you had children
-It's like you wanted the world to punish them
-And you painted the picture that everyone else
was being cruel
-When the truth is all bad things point back to
you
- I'll never understand why you can't take
accountability for what you've done
-Now you're confused on why you have none of
your kids love
-A mother huh...that's what you want to be
-But you couldn't even manage to take care of
your responsibilities
-Yet you still win because you've made me waste
all my time
-Instead of taking care of myself I have you on
my mind
-Now i'm falling behind
- I so desperately want to rewind
-Every encounter before I met you, cause things
were fine
-I can't say perfect that doesn't exist
-The minute I was born I was destined for
conflict
-But it's everyone else's fault right

-Even though you carried me, made every
decision, birthed me, it's on them I almost died
-The absolute worst part about everything
-Is that all your narratives you actually believe
-I hope one day you start to realize
-You are what led to this demise
-Ill never understand why you had children
Its like you wanted the world to be mean to them
_you painted this picture that everyone else was
being cruel
When all bad things point back to you
-what you're doing is selfish and getting out of
hand
So when I cut you off
I hope you're not telling yourself ,"I'll never
understand"

What Is Love?

You showed me love was pain,
Not a feeling I could gain.
Love is the one feeling I can never share,
You never showed me how
You were never there.
I disrespect those, I cannot live without,
I let the ones in who hurt me, without a doubt.
You are supposed to be my leader, my example.
Can't you show me love, even just a sample?
Monkey do what Monkey see.
Tag, I'm it.
Can't you see?
I HURT THEM BECAUSE
YOU….HURT…..ME!!!
I hurt the one person, who stays on my mind.
One by one, over my wall,
I leave them all,
behind.
Unless that's the secret about love, you just
never showed me.
You give them love, you give them many,
But you don't give your daughters any!
You have sons, who don't have a father.
We're never getting your love, so why do I
bother?

All these kids you created,
Since we're clearly not loved, I guess we're all
hated.
Missed date, after missed date.
I don't want your love,
I'd rather keep your hate.

The Thing About Angels

All babies cry
So imagine my surprise
When I held him, looked into his eyes
And he would not cry
Every heart beats
So imagine my defeat
When I listened to his chest
And the beat didn't repeat
All births are beautiful
Bringing a baby in this world is a miracle
And I knew this would forever change my life
But all babies cry
All except mine
Every heart beats
But his didn't do anything
Birth is beautiful
But it wasn't that night
I never expected my baby to not survive
The deep pain of a mother outliving their child
I held the lifeless body in my hands
For once in my life I didn't understand God's
plans
No one teaches you how to properly grieve
I thought to myself this must be him punishing
me

Nothing hurts more than knowing we will never
meet
I touch my stomach with a permanent reminder
That I lost the only thing proving I was a fighter
This moment would always be my biggest
heartbreak
An endless feeling that I will never shake
Because I am still here and my baby is not
I have an aching heart and the pain won't stop
Just imagine my surprise, when I looked into his
eyes
And had to accept defeat, when his heart
wouldn't beat
I had to learn it just wasn't my time and one day
I will have that beautiful night

Pause Now Go

-Time passed by and you were still on top of me
-Cant this time go faster so I could be free
-Time went faster and it continued longer
-I could not fight because you were way stronger
-All your friends stood there as they watched
and applauded
-Wait...Pause
-Now go…back to the animal did you really
have to hurt me?
-Did you have to continue on even after my
plea?
-You really hurt me is that something you can't
see?
-Then you told your friends they couldn't
anything
-So as It continued my heart throbbed
-But wait ...pause
-Now go …..back to my dad will you ever
respond
-Will we start to have an actual bond
-Wait. Pause
-Now go ..back to my love will you finally lower
your lever
-Or will our future be erased forever
-Pause to the guy who held me down

-Pause to my dad who left me with a frown
-Pause to my love who might be left in the past
-Pause to you all because I will move on so fast
-Time will continue it'll go by so slow
-You'll try to apologize but I will turn and say no
-SO JUST PAUSE….NOW GO

Puppet Master

In the puppet master a truth is revealed
One only i can see to the rest its concealed
So i watch as the show unfolds
The puppets refuse to hear a truth that needs to
be told
For the master doesn't care who is severed
Or that this is something you'll regret forever
They couldn't fight my battle cause it got in the
way of yours
but now you're in pain so that's all they are good
for
They were a burden to you back then
And now you want them marching in with the
head of your villain
They can all fight for you since they lost their
fight in me
Who knew your inconvenience brought
everyone to knees
Your pulling the strings of a bunch of angry
minds
Deep down knowing nothing will make it fine
I thought the joke was on you
So why am i left looking like a fool
I'm thinking i can save him though
And they are the farthest one down the tightrope

He's prince charming but i don't know how to be
saved
And I can't protect him from you attacking his
grace
Round of applause for the puppet master
But i'll severe the ties that bound us, if he
doesn't return after
You called the battle the line has been drawn
To death someones gonna fall

Five Ws And H

How could I speak when someone takes my
voice
How could I be happy when someone takes my
joy
How can I trust someone when they lie to my
face
How can I be free when someone takes all my
space
What is the point of having someone there
What is the point of breathing this toxic air
Why would I listen to all these "helping" voices
around me
Why would I present myself if no one can see
When would I be released from all this pain
When would I finally break this chain
Who could ever be that person I run to
Who could ever be that person to drag me from
what I'm going
through
Where would I go to share my words
Where would I go to fly with the birds
Where, what, why,......Who, when, how
Trying to be strong when everyone lets me down
Where, what, why,......Who, when, how
Time to leave the stage, time to take a bow

Where, what, why,......Who, when, how
A victim back then, a survivor now

Dear Guy

Dear guy, how do you sleep at night?
 Knowing that you caused so much fright
Do you toss and turn with guilt and shame,
Or do you sleep soundly, without any blame?
Do you ever think about the people you hurt,
The lives you shattered, the tears you spurred?
 Or do you just go about your day, as if nothing
happened, nothing to say?
Do you have a heart, a conscience, a soul,
Or are you just an empty, hollow hole?
Do you ever feel remorse or regret, Or do you
just forget, move on, and let?
Dear guy, I hope you find a way,
To make amends, to change your ways.
To see the error of your past,
For sleep is not just a physical need,
It's a state of mind, a chance to heed.
To the voice within, that tells you right,
Dear guy, how do you sleep at night?

Secret Garden

It's just a helpless bee
First opportunity and you were ready to sting
A beanstalk even jack won't climb
You're the giants greatest demise
Now u Play the cards of compare and contrast
When we both know they never treated me like
that
Never had to say who was right who was wrong
Mature enough to admit we both had our flaws
Go Ahead plant the seeds of truth
We don't need the seeds to know id choose them
over you
I don't know why you place them on a lower
level
Because they would never have me dancing with
the devil
See I'm feeling a bit like Adam, still guilty of
biting a fruit he didn't take
Like I'm guilty of a fixing a heart I didn't break
I guess that makes you Eve
Listening to a snake just to mess up everything
The poison of your roots killed my garden
I should be happy that everything blown free
But now i'm stuck with a plant that don't mean a
thing

I must rebuild this foundation I hardened
All because I let weeds impose on
The secrets of my garden

Take it from me

-Take it from me
-I know it might be harder to believe
-Just speaking from experience
-Heres a few hints incase you're curious
-If they wanted to give you a kiss they would have done it
-To you their everything and to them you're not shit
-I'm just saying, I've dealt with the pain
-Take it from me so you don't go down that lane
-The sweet little nothings
-To stray from the fussing
-And the hypnosis smile
-That only leads you to an endless mile
-Take it from me, first hand advice
-Don't be thrown around like some game board dice
-Take it from me since no one else will
-Or at least not you. So ill take the intellectual feel

Mute

-We're expecting to get by
-With a speechless hi
-And the assumption that were on the same page
-When really one of us don't feel the same way
-Yet we still let silence fill the room
-Telling me how to feel for you
-So I wait and wait for it to become night
-Because that's when I know everything will be alright
-We talk until 12am ,I finally feel like yours
-In this moment I know I don't have to worry anymore
-But morning comes, I dread the day ahead
-Instead of talking were sitting on opposite ends
-Both waiting to see who'll talk first
-Making me lose more of my self-worth
-If not to speak, what are conversations for
-But im too scared
-By protecting my heart, I risk not gaining yours

Hidden love language

Hidden love language
Whats your love language
A question I came to regret?
Cause you said all of them
After all this time I have not seen one yet..
Words Of Affirmation...Easy
I boost up your confidence and encourage you
all the time
And in return you tell me I can't do anything
right
So im guessing that love language isn't yours
Which is okay..there are four more
Quality time..
You always say there are more important things
to do
Then why would I clear my whole schedule for
you?
Now were down to three.....
Physical touch that must be your thing
You touch and touch..yet I dont want your hands
on me
But you said I have to makeup for not being
pretty
Just two..
Acts of service you relate to the most

I do anything you want..but for my activities you
go ghost
When's the last time we did something I liked?
We never have, never will..and you find that
alright?
On our last one what are the odds
Gift giving is your love language after all
You found this person you wanna give
everything to
Just to discover they aren't even thinking about
you
I gave away the best gift..my heart
Not knowing I never had yours in the start
There must be a sixth love language
Something to explain whats caused this damage
I just need a reason behind what you do
Or to understand why I was never enough for
you
So ill just tell myself theres another love
language
To put myself at ease
Because I cant tell myself that you were not
made for me
Theres a sixth love language that makes you feel
you dont have to try
And makes you enjoy a relationship of tears and
lies
That puts us in a place where all we do is fight
There's another love language...right?

I keep going back to not being enough
You have a love language...But not someone you
love

Heart Of A Mind

We're told to Think with your head not your
heart
So we go and set those things apart
I Listen to my mind
Because my heart will make me go blind
There is something they want me to see
My heart… no my mind knows what's best for
me
My mind takes me back to when our anniversary
was set
But my heart takes me back to when we first met
My mind will let me know something is aching
My heart will let me know that it is breaking
My mind is wondering what we're doing this for
But my heart is saying it can't take anymore
You must think with your head not your heart
But they are both saying you're a work of art
My heart no my mind destroyed this masterpiece
When they finally agree I feel so relieved
I no longer have a heart
And I've lost my mind
I'm guessing that's why we're finally out of time

Do you want to play a game

Do you want to play a game?
 I was a kid of course I did
The question that led to the worst thing someone
can commit
Lets play a tickle game, we have to find every
ticklish spot
However you stayed tickling one spot alot
Only I got tickled, when was it your turn?
But the more you tickled, the more I learned
The next time we played doctor but I didn't feel
sick
But you reassured me I needed to be fully
examined
We played a bunch of games, you had all the
touching roles
As I got older the games were more out of
control
Finally we played a new one
Although the end results could never be undone
Not enough games could make this one
equivalent
In this game you took my innocence
Now were playing a game, a game of life
Where I get a baby except its gonna die
Another tally added to a game I didn't win

Leaving me the one to suffer with the
punishment
Then I created a game
Putting all of yours to shame
Lets see how far the knife goes in-
Finally I got a win
Never regretted a second, it fed my pride
That was until you won the game because you
actually survived
Its unfair im the one who has a body full of scars
Only to find myself the one behind bars
After all the playing I was never the same
Wish I would've said I didn't want to play a
game

The clock strikes

The clock strikes 12
And I'm calling you fairytale
Now it's hit 1
And we're nowhere near done
The clock now reads 2
You're telling me everything we've been through
Its finally reached 3
We're discussing future dreams
We stop at hour 4
Even though im impatient to hear more
The hand hits 5
I get to hear more about your life
Time flies its now 6
And i'm wondering how I don't remember any of
it
We moved on to hour 7
All I can think about is your presence
Who cares if the time is now 8
When I'm catching up with my soulmate
Then its finally 9
Im brought back from my made up paradise
My smile fades it's now turni 10
I will make it my goal to never forget this again
We finally reached 11
I send my final prayer to heaven

Forgetting a loved one that should be a sin
Yet you still constantly let me in
You're stuck dating a broken mind
I wouldn't blame you if you left this all behind
I can let this sickness take every other part of me
But I will not let you be a forgotten memory
Returning from this I wish would have died
But I know everything will be okay the minute
the clock strikes

Every last thing

Every last thing I wanted to say
You took it and stripped my words away
Something so big that was apart of my life
I can't share all because you said goodbye?
Maybe I'm the fool
For coming back to you
But then doesn't that make you one too..
Every last thing I wanted to say
Hidden in the poems you don't want me to make
And what about the others who have had their
heart broken?
They have no one to relate to because my words
have been stolen
My poetry never changed just the people within
You turned a bright light into one dim
Utterly selfish, was this the best I can do
Are these really the standards I hold myself to
Flashing your smile to make everything alright
But I am tired of putting up a fight
I am willingly holding the door open for you
Don't you want me out of your life too?
I can't stand to see that look in your eyes

New kind Of Body

I got a real man now
One that brings a smile to the face you made
frown
Taking hands off the body you held down
Healing a heart he didn't break
Giving back innocence to a girl he didn't rape
I got a real man now
That's something you can never be
Something you knew was never a possibility
Cause your a coward
Crying to your parents to fix your problems
Mommy and Daddy can't buy you this
You can't make a man out of something so
worthless
I don't understand how you sleep at night
Knowing little girls is what you call your type
And you go above the law because you don't get
your way
Yet somehow you convinced yourself this was
okay
It takes about 28 days for skin cells to replace
themselves
That means I finally have a body you didn't
touch
No reminders of the fact no one gave you love

I have a body where things happen because I
said so
Not a broken body because you don't know the
word no
So yeah you may be the reason I have
nightmares here and there
A reason why I say life isn't fair
But you're done being the reason I'm broken
down
You see I got a real man now

Writers Revenge

They plead for me to "Stop Writing!"
Those words are so delighting
To see you so fearful of what is being said
Everything you've done to me, you now dread
You realize you no longer have power over me
Holding on to that weapon of silencing
But I will write again and tell everyone about you
I'll make sure the world knows what you put me through
You're banishing the hands that tell the story of who you are
These truths will set a higher bar
Traits that you will never be able to meet
And oh how I love that you see your defeat
"Stop Writing!".. please you continue to beg
What can't I expose? Why are you so afraid?
"Stop Writing!" Or at least let me tell my part
But you have been writing this narrative from the start
Ive been sick of all the fighting!
I want this to be an ugly sighting!
Your words have been so binding!
For that..I'll never stop writing!

Siren

I can hear the siren…
I can hear them coming
I can hear the siren
But still, I remain silent
Diagnosed with craziness
Life has been such a mess
Wish this could be over now
I just want to rest
Can you hear my voice, Can you hear my call
Can you hear me yell, banging on the walls
One minute I was standing, then found lying on the floor
I heard my sisters' cry, when they ran through the door
Then it finally happened, my arms began to shake
My body had its own earthquake
I saw my sisters fall to the ground
My beloved sisters crying, praying out loud
Then it all turned black, I saw nothing more
I woke up wondering, what was I in the ambulance for?
It was then, I realized the reigns were no longer mine.

The thief had struck again. My puppeteer for the win.
A seizure had taken my body, but I stole it right back.
While in the hospital, they called. They seemed to care.
All it took was a near-death experience to remind my "parents,"
I was actually "theirs."
They asked, "why didn't you call to tell us what was going on?"
So you want me to call a stranger? One, I never even see? Go on!
A few days later, I can hear the siren
I see my sisters crying
I could hear the siren
Wonder who could it be
I could hear the siren
OH NO ITS FOR ME
I could hear the siren
But I still remain silent
I could hear the siren
HAIL MARY-HAIL MARY, Who lost a loved one now
Hail Mary-Who could it be?
HAIL MARY-HAIL MARY, will it be me?

My Manipulator

Manipulatively
You ask me to do things flashing me puppy dog
eyes
And shockingly to your surprise
I will say yes and do it all for you
When in reality there's nothing I wouldn't do
Manipulatively
You break me down, then turn it on me
As if there's no chance in the world you can be a
possibility
Each of your words sings a lullaby in my head
What was actually your fault became mine
instead
Manipulatively
You got me wrapped around your finger
What hurts more about being a doubter is being
a true believer
Constantly having to defend what no one else
sees
But the whole time you blinded me
Manipulatively
You should be ashamed
To treat someone like a toss up game
How did it feel to pull all the strings?
How did it feel to do it all... Manipulatively

The A

Teachers are so quick to tell you something
about your work
Not knowing school is the last thing on your
mind and that's adding on to your hurt
See they will rage at you for having missing
assignments
When you're focused on daddy not coming
home last night
Teachers will get angry when you're always late
While you're focused on helping mom get food
on your plate
Teachers are stuck on something that can be
turned in on a later day
And you're still wondering why your sister ran
away
So daddy never came home, no food on the
plate, sister ran away
And " focus on your work" is all you got to
say?...
Mommy and Daddy are fighting…... but let me
do this essay
Let me do this math equation instead of
convincing mom to stay
Because every A is worth additional pain

Got 100% but now my cousin is leaving on a
plane
Cried myself to sleep my whole world turned
gray
But hey...least I got an A
An a is all that matters to a teacher the most
Never worried on how your student tried to
overdose
So they come to school and you go off because
things aren't turned in
And that was it you melted the ice that was
already thin
So they sit there and think of home and school
While you go home thinking everything is cool
Next day you take attendance they're absent
A few weeks later you find out they're laying six
feet under in their casket
See cause daddy never came home, there was no
food on the plate
Sister ran away, and cousin left on the plane
Mom and dad are fighting, they're trying to
convince mom to stay
On top of all that they no longer have that A
So your death gave mom insurance, there's food
on the plate
Your cousin, dad, and sister came back and
never went away
You turned in your assignments, after all that
was your whole aim

But now you're dead…………..Hey...At Least
You got That A

www.ingramcontent.com/pod-product-compliance
Lightning Source LLC
LaVergne TN
LVHW010828200726
843508LV00012B/2531